Halina Rarot

Literary Pictures of Kyiv

Great Britain, London 2022

Publisher: Anna Maria Mickiewicz Literary Waves London 2022

Author: Halina Rarot

Editor: Anna Maria Mickiewicz

Translation: Anna Maria Mickiewicz

Stan Mickiewicz

Steve Rushton

Cover design: Agnieszka Herman

Photo by Stan Mickiewicz

Photos by Stan Mickiewicz

ISBN 9798834822202

The following philosophical essay about Kyiv was written at a good and wonderful time for Ukraine in 2012 at the beginning of the third decade of building independence and after the author's intense scientific and personal contacts with Ukrainian philosophers from Kyiv, meeting Viktor Malakhov from the Institute of Philosophy of the Ukrainian Academy of Sciences and Anatoliy Tikholaz from the Mohyla Academy at scientific conferences and in summer or winter events of Lublin-Kyiv friends, thanks to whom it was possible to fall in love with "beautiful, golden

Kyiv", enjoying its architecture and European character. It was also a time of longing for another trip, to be able to carelessly stroll around Khreschatyk again, visit churches, buy paintings in Andriyivskyy Spusk, bathe in the Dnipro, visit the hospitable home of the Tikholaz family in Grape Alley or the Malakhov's home on Mayakovsky Prospect, listen to their dreams about a bright future for Ukraine, plan the next stages of scientific co-operation between Lublin and Kyiv. Then, in 2014, the essay was reprinted as a small booklet and supplemented with sentences on the *Orange Revolution*, later known as the *Revolution of Dignity*. Already then, Lublin's friends were worried about their beloved Kyiv, watching the news photos of fighting in Maidan, when black smoke from burning tyres rose over Kyiv. And dramatically, this essay needs updating again. But what's happening now in Ukraine and Kyiv forces us to silence. Silence itself, as is well known, has many meanings. Certainly, deep sadness is silent, while the little sorrows are talkative, as Seneca used to say. Silence can also be a great accusation. Unspeakable words are louder than the sound of a drum said Huan-zi. Let silence then ring! Let great souls bear the suffering of Kyiv in silence.

And let a bright thread of hope shine through this black silence, more and more visible to us every day.

Halina Rarot

Kyiv like a sailing ship

To begin with, to look at a literary-poetic image of the city based on Irina Matkowska's analysis of the medieval anonymous epic *The Tale of Igor's Campaign* (about the expedition of Prince Igor Sviatoslavovich against the Polovtsy), looking for a picture of Kyiv presented in the epic not only as the centre of Old Russian territory but also as a living heart that reacts emotionally to all events taking place in its native land. The defeat of Igor and his army caused the city to freeze with grief. It is therefore the personification of the collective heart of the Ruthenian land. This is the first time the Ukrainian mentality is revealed with its primacy of the order of the heart, in later times resulting in cord centrism – a strictly Ukrainian philosophy.

However, the city of Kyiv cannot be reduced to its ancient history. There are also histories and images from the nineteenth century, from the 1940s and 1960s, left in letters by Józef Ignacy Kraszewski. Kyiv seen through his eyes was above all a city of free trade between landowners and bourgeoisie, meetings of the most eminent citizens from all over Ukraine, Volhynia, Podolia and Lithuania. In these numerous conferences for business it was not only about buying or selling property, buying food products for the whole year or luxury items, not only about investing capital, or taking out the necessary loan, but also about spending time happily at feasts and balls, at which…

> "The wine was flowing in a stream, and thousands fell on the green tables, one card often killing a whole fortune and sometimes even a good name".

It is also Kyiv from the beginning of the 20th century, best rendered by Vasyl Rozanov, who, as a Russian, admired it, seeing it as the noblest city in Russia, free from the severity and stubbornness typical of Muscovites, from the recklessness and superficiality (on the one hand) and the melancholy and severity (on the other) of residents of St. Petersburg. The people of Kyiv, in his portrait, recorded in the sketch *Kijew i kijewlanie*, were different from the inhabitants of Russian Warsaw (as it was) –less neat, attentive, and hospitable than Kyivians.

Kyiv reminded Rozanov of ancient Mycenae, different from the whole of Hellas. The Russian writer and philosopher sees the obvious effects of former Kyiv saints' influence on the city's spirit, freeing it forever from the typical sinfulness of every large city centre. Moscow, in his opinion, will never be an innocent city, and St. Petersburg will never be joyful. Simply put, Kyiv is a lump of gold on the Earth. And the ultimate support for all of Russia that will make Russia die in two or three millennia thinking "I will go to Kyiv, and if I do not regain my strength there, it will be easier for me to at least leave this world."

It is also Kyiv from the period of World War II and the first post-war years, shown in the poetry of the Ukrainian poet Maksym Rylski (1895-1964), in the poems *I lost my words ... Is there a limit?* Despair, anger, anger at the destruction of a city and overwhelming fear felt in post-war Kyiv causing the entire body to die, intertwined, as researcher Ludmila Siryk analyzes, with hopes for the future of Ukraine.

Kyiv, its recent past and present, are visible in the philosophy and essays of W. Małachow. He is the initiator of ideas, such as in the album *Polish addresses of Kijewo*, and in his statement entitled *Kijewskije miedytacyi* (Kyiv meditations, 2005), a kind of artistic prose focusing on a somewhat secretive love for the city:

> "How St. Vladimir in the past erects his cross over a great river and almost like a huge ship, sparkling with thousands of lights, sails our city somewhere in the distance, into the Ukrainian steppes. What can stop this sumptuous movement? Wars came and went, they died like an old beggar, immortal riots, with a black apocalyptic string, Chernobyl rang and froze, melted in the disturbing, swollen clouds above us, and the city sailed - Szczekawica and Chorewica and the wonderful Starokijowska Góra and the golden Pechersk and the widely scattered Padół, and white massifs catching up with each other, white on gray, gray on green – it sailed ...

"What is Kyiv? A riddle, or rather a mystery, a mystery covered with silence. The silence is mysterious, if only because it's unusual for the southern city of Kyiv. Silent and enigmatic in a spiritual feat, in an immeasurable gentleness, are the young holy princes Boris and Gleb, the martyrs in whom Kyivan Rus' prophetically saw an ideal of holiness; the lifestyle of inhabitants of Pechersk is quiet and concentrated; silent are the delights of the flame burners who have waited for centuries in the hot and bright sun to bow down to these holy places; quietly, leaving almost no trace, we cross the Kyiv valleys and hills of the century; quietly, with accompanying myriad fires and sounds, our city sails like a ship."

The city as sailing ship gives us much food for thought. One of the meanings will be, of course, the immersion of the stronghold of Vladimir the Great in the vast Ukrainian steppes, as if into the waves of the sea. As the author writes further in his Kyiv meditations, and he is aware of it, there are centres or city centres whose beauty and charm we perceive at once, and cities where we fall in love slowly. As for Kyiv itself, it is easy to equate its image, apart from the strong visual silence, with the hills of Transnistria and golden domes, hastily calling it "Golden Kyiv". On the other hand, Małachow sees it as a small universe full of diversity and uniqueness. Each part of this universe has its own original rhythm and style, its metaphysics and epistemology – after all, Pechersk cannot be seen in the same way as Newki or Lipki.

Lipki: proud, full of power and seriousness, the walls of solid houses raised over the city. The spirit of place, like a great grey bird, carefully guards its spaces, able to expand only due to acquired, nostalgic longing. From Lipki, along the Dnieper hill, there are thoughtful parks, filled with the sun, the brilliance of water, and the changing sapphire of Kyiv; they reveal themselves, so as not to disappear. Around the next bend there are secluded dating sites, in the green of chestnut trees and acacia everything becomes brighter and, in the end, we are completely enveloped in the sparkling, unreal beauty of palaces, churches, a space imbued with concrete and painfully delightful details of the riverside oikumene. And even lower and to the left, stretching towards the Obołońskie meadows, the Paddle roars and chatters, always worried about something, poor and enterprising, combining the southern coastal turmoil with the dignity of an average place, full of antiquities and silence. Triumphant in its central squares, now here the truncated square of old walls, stalls, wagons, ship's sides being dug up, but beyond all this rusting strip, as if gaining energy to detach and fly, the new, great Kyiv is already preparing for a run-in; a city of highways and bridges and white massifs catching up with each other on the horizon. Kyiv, remembered by the elusive face of St. Sofia on the windshield of a car racing away.

Getting to know the "little Kyiv homeland", its style, spirit and history, based on this method, the literary image, becomes, according to Małachow, a real basis for (re-) building identity, as well as a source of local patriotism and moral attitudes. The author argues that failure to care for the unique face and atmosphere of a place of residence inevitably leads to a standardization of human life.

I will briefly refer to my own contribution to the philosophy (epistemology) of this city, which is the already cited article in Ukrainian, *Tuga za*

Kyjewom (with the Polish name *Longing for Kiev*). Like W. Małachow, I use the method of the literary image to describe Kyiv. We are different, however, in grasping the basics of these images: the Ukrainian philosopher makes it an actively lived love, because following Max Scheler, he believes that only this kind of feeling is a flawless way to learn values.

However, I consider the theme of longing for the lost city of Kyiv, for I assume that longing, although it is one of the components of love, is a wider feeling than love (you can miss what you have not seen or had).

J. Iwaszkiewicz, born and raised in Ukraine (in 1894, in Kalnik in the Kyiv province) wrote his first novel (an autobiography) when he became a Polish exile in Warsaw. Filled with longing (the only sincere feeling) for Ukraine and Kyiv, he saw his youthful city in his waking dreams:

> "Echoes of the early rains of the early season and your shadows old, old, old town. Surrounded by the green of spring veils, surrounded by gardens, domes, listening to those spring bells (...) sometimes in the

evening, tired of our city; buildings, terraces, streets climbing upwards like hanging New York bridges, bright April trees, monasteries with blue, blue domes, the slopes of church gardens over the grey bedding of the waters."

It is impossible not to refer to the most recent times of this city, reflected in other literary pictures not included in the above-mentioned works. In *Pis'my iz Kijewa* (*Letters from Kiev*), which appeared in the columns of the *Gorożanin* weekly, their author Natalia Szelipova stating that the modern heart of the Kiev metropolis is the metro, a unique communication artery living its life and at the same time subordinating the entire city to itself, transporting one million seven hundred thousand people a day, making them dependent on each other, determining the value of the apartment, the meeting place, the choice of book to read, the manner of suicide or the time of the last kiss. As soon as we go underground, we satisfy the need to participate in the life of this city, and the exit from the metro becomes the same as the ritual of cleansing.

In the vicinity of the metro, an alternative underground shopping centre Metropolis has been built in Kyiv. Contrary to the underground, dark side present in every human being, full of chaos and unpredictability, the underground, two-level part of the city is well thought out and ordered, located near the centre of Kyiv, with six separate zones (Turkey, Italy, France, Ukraine, Poland and Germany) each containing commercial products of that country. In this alternative city are fountains with stands surrounding them where you can throw money into the water.

In addition to the heart, Kyiv, like every city, also has its own conciliar mind (an agora, a place of debates and stormy, revolutionary births of new ideas, especially in the political dimension) – Independence Square, which the whole world has unanimously called, since the Orange Revolution, Majdan, and after the tragic winter events of 2014, Euromaidan. There are monuments to the Ukrainian Founding Fathers, symbols of national independence, and here the blood of martyrs shed in the fight for free choice for Ukrainian civilization and affiliation. It is a place of Ukrainian hope, pride, honour and blood. It is a place which will be reborn again to wake tourists, as always, with the rich architecture of Khreschatyk Street, a Kyiv of recent years clearly influenced by hybrid postmodern architectural aesthetics. Glocalisation tendencies are connected with ideas of reflective modernization, combining the old and new in one living whole, Kyiv itself. As the recognized media theorist Lev Manowich writes in his fundamental work *The Language of New Media*, such logic makes European cities modern and at the same time full of life, the architectural styles of many epochs intertwining with postmodern architecture, Mediterranean time (or precisely Kyiv time) meeting internet time. This is what the bustling Khreschatyk is like, this is how the square is slowly becoming.

Kontraktowy was also affected by the transformations of the urban space of Kiev, by the preparations for Euro 2012. As Oleksij Radynski writes in the article *Polityczna geography of Kiev*, the reconstruction of Kontraktowy Square takes place under the slogan "return to the sources", to restore the "original" (commercial) functions of historical buildings located on this square.

Elements of the axiology of the city of Kyiv

The essence of Kyiv is not only its infrastructure, its architecture, whether Old Russian, modern, postmodern, above-ground or underground. It is also made up of people who for generations have been formulating the mentality of Kyivans, outlined in the philosophy and literature of previous centuries. It can be painstakingly found in the works of Kiev poets, writers and philosophers: in Ilarion, Grigory Skovoroda, Mikołaj Gogol, Mikołaj Bierdiajew, Mikhail Bulgakov, Wilen Gorski and many others. One can also find its synthesis, an insight into the axiological structure of inner, spiritual Kyiv, in a certain style of interpersonal relations, in types of thinking, in the type of Kyivan spirituality, in their intellectual and moral life, giving rise to thinking systems, new lifestyles. Here is how the Kiev mentality is perceived by W.Malakhov:

> "It is a structure of the mind which, following Wadim Skuratowski, can and should be associated with Kyiv's disappointment with history, adopting a healthy and positive perspective. A characteristic feature of this type of mentality is undoubtedly that it strives for the ideal of integrity of existence, and at the same time is free from the utopianism of projects to repair the world, the mania to implement them, to bring things to an end. The Kyiv intellectual is rather a dreamer and an ironist, existentially an individualist, but this individualism means seeking the centre, because it's directed at the desired and impossible integration of what cannot even be named. That is why the Kyiv intellectual will silently devote his life to what does not exist, what has been forgotten, the traces and advantages of which can only be joked about with friends; it is in this style, in this taste."

This Kyiv, sometimes a salutary inability to bring matters to an end, can be found, for example, in the novel *Master and Margarita* by the great writer from Kyiv, Mikhail Bulgakov. A Ukrainian writer from the beginning of the 20th century wanted to present the Christian idea of a fight between good and evil without using violence. According to S.W. Krymskij, another famous philosopher from Kiev:

> "Matthew the Levite, wishing to save Yeshua Ha Nocri from shameful death, did not make it to Golgotha. From the neighbouring hill he watches the crucifixion of his Teacher and curses God: You terrible God! Why am I late? Likewise, Margaret comes to the Master with the intention of staying with him forever. But she is losing her fatal delay of just a few minutes."

Analyzing the problem of new spiritual needs in an individualized contemporary world, he sees here rather a weakness of good which is almost deliberately late, because it could lose much of its original purity in direct contact with evil forces. In my opinion, however, there is a most visible flawed utopianism in Kyivian philosophy, an inevitable disappointment, crying with regret "why am I late?" Another and most modern example confirming the existence of the Kyiv structure of the mind is the events of recent years. Well, in the oldest part of the city there is the Gonczary forest, surrounded by hills, turned off and inaccessible for everyday viewing or tourist exploration. As O. Radynski writes, a well-known Ukrainian architect proposed the idea of transforming this place into a "monument to 19th century town planning and national crafts". It would then synthesize a thousand-year history of the district, famous for many crafts, especially pottery and trade, as part of the valley. The fake atmosphere and spirit of the 11th century would appear here, created by people dressed as the inhabitants of medieval Kyiv, producing dishes, baking bread, forging metal, cutting trees or weaving linen. The visiting tourists could watch them, but also make pottery themselves. This postmodern project began, as Radynski ironically states, with the installation of the achievements of modern civilization, i.e. a gas pipeline and sewage system in the wilderness. It ended there too. When one writes about any place in the axiological aspect, one also takes into account the beauty of its morality and the ugliness of immorality, and emphasizes that, especially in large cities, phenomena testifying to social pathology occur on a large scale. In the case of Kyiv, even when choosing a distanced view, free from longing or love, it is difficult to find it and then describe dirt, crime, or even weak religiosity.

For Kyiv is still a holy city, marked by the baptism of Rus, by Prince Vladimir entrusting it to the protection of the Mother of God in 989. It is even built like Jerusalem ("New Jerusalem"), as evidenced by the Golden Gates, resembling those through which Christ entered Jerusalem. The Kyiv-Pechersk Lavra, the former heart of this city, is a place where, in addition to tourists, numerous pilgrimages still come. This unusualness of the inhabitants of Kyiv translates into their everyday attitudes: into their great sympathy and protectiveness towards dogs and pigeons. As the author of Letters from Kyiv writes, "the other peculiarity of Kyiv is pigeons. I don't know why, but they got rid of all fear of people."

Conclusion

At the end of this article, I express two hopes: one related directly to the description of Kiev itself, the other related to the possibility of philosophical reflection on the phenomenon of the city in general. I expect my description will one day be supplemented with an image of Kiev in the poetry of the "Silver Age", in the works of Kiev neo-classicists (in literature) or with philosophical approaches such as: "Contemporary Kyiv – an outline of political hermeneutics", "Kiev architecture as a cultural phenomenon". Or anthropological and cultural considerations such as "Kiev - the eternal city", "Kyiv and Rome: similarities and differences. (Should Kyiv be the eternal city?)" In W. Małachow's opinion, each city (Saint Petersburg, Kyiv or Ostróg) in its own way leads to the same thought:

"It is very important and valuable for modern man to maintain a vivid feeling of belonging to a small family, to feel and understand the uniqueness of place, where we loved, enjoyed, suffered and where, perhaps, we will die. The spirit of this place is always ready to embrace us with its indescribable serenity, so that we can only be careful and attentive towards it and not try to violate what has been created and expressed not by us. After all, it is not only the works of nature and the mementos of human hands that are fragile. Perhaps even more fragile are the unique cultural phenomena that have arisen over centuries that make Paris, Ostróg and Kyiv what they are. It is difficult to define them. It is easy to destroy them, to cover their internal structure with darkness. They have their lifelong layers, not always subordinate to man and society. (Otherwise how would they reward us in our dark times?)"

As for philosophical reflections on the phenomenon of the city in general, I think that relying on literary images is the most effective method in relation to the philosophy of individual "places" and "cities" and – what is more – this fits with "pictorial thinking" which is becoming more and more popular today.

From the Editor

Books published by the London-based Anna Maria Mickiewicz Literary Waves Publishing:

Błaszak Danuta, Mickiewicz Anna Maria [w]: *Do zobaczenia 2*, Literary Waves (London 2021), ISBN 978-1-63901-856-7

Fert Józef Franciszek: *The Life of Cyprian Norwid (1821-1883),* Literary Waves Publishing, red. Anna Maria Mickiewicz, tłumaczenie: Urszula Błaszak, Stanisław Mickiewicz, Steve Rushton, (London 2021), ISBN-13: 979-8516176869

Mickiewicz Anna Maria (red.) [w]: *Krzysztof Kamil Baczyński Poet of the Warsaw Uprising 1944 Poeta Powstania Warszawskiego 1944 Saved poetry, manuscripts, and drawings Poezja, rękopisy i rysunki ocalone*, Literary Waves Publishing, (London 2021), tłumaczenie: Anna Maria Mickiewicz, Tomasz Mickiewicz, Steve Rushton, ISBN 978-1-7947-1902-6

Danuta Błaszak, Anna Maria Mickiewicz [w]: *Atlantyckie strofy. Współcześni poeci z USA i Wielkiej Brytanii,* wydanie: pierwsze, (Londyn 2020), Literary Waves Publishing, ISBN: 978-83-957749-5-9

Sławiński Alex [w]: *Counting to Four Poems*, (London 2020), Literary Waves Publishing, ISBN:979-8587225

Mickiewicz Anna Maria red. [w]: *Mathematics versus Poetry*, Literary Waves Publishing, (London 2022), ISBN 979-8404012835

Lizakowski Adam [w]: Gdybym twą miłość miał Ameryko! Wybór wierszy, Literary Waves Publishing, Londyn 2022, ISBN 978-1-4583-7869-9

Mickiewicz Anna Maria (red.), Błaszak Danuta (red.) [w]: Antologia *Walizka z literami, Twórczość pisarzy emigracyjnych 2022, (Wielka Brytania, USA, Australia, Niemcy, Brazylia, Francja, Izrael, Belgia, Irlandia i Norwegia)*, Literary Waves Publishing, ISBN 978-1-4583-8370-9, London 2022

Editor: Mickiewicz Anna Maria [w]: Anthology *Ukraine in the work of international poets (Ukraine, Australia, Bulgaria, Israel, Poland, UK, USA)*, Literary Waves Publishing, PoEzja Londyn, London 2022, ISBN 978-1-4583-5727-4

Krzysztof Kamil Baczyński Poet of the Warsaw Uprising 1944 Saved poetry, manuscripts, and drawings, Literary Waves Publishing, (London 2022), translated by: Anna Maria Mickiewicz, Tomasz Mickiewicz, Steve Rushton, Stan Mickiewicz, ISBN 979-8802065853

contact: anna_mickiewicz@yahoo.co.uk

Printed in Great Britain
by Amazon

81683442R00020